A Sackful of Limericks

Michael Palin

Illustrations by Tony Ross

BOOKS

3 5 7 9 10 8 6 4 2

Random House Books
20 Vauxhall Bridge Road
London SW1V 2SA

Random House Books is part of the Penguin Random
House group of companies whose addresses can be
found at global.penguinrandomhouse.com.

Penguin
Random House
UK

Many of the limericks in this collection first
appeared in Michael Palin's *Limericks*.

First edition published by Hutchinson in 1985
This edition published by Random House Books in 2016

www.penguin.co.uk

A CIP catalogue record for this book is
available from the British Library.

ISBN 9781847947994

Printed and bound by Clays Ltd, St Ives plc

Penguin Random House is committed to a sustainable future
for our business, our readers and our planet. This book is
made from Forest Stewardship Council® certified paper.

Introduction to the new edition

As the old saying goes, a limerick is for life, and not just for Christmas. But there is something festive about this particular literary form, and I've always thought their natural home might be inside a cracker, wrapped around those cosy little gifts like self-assembling ear-rings and plastic thumbscrews. No cracker company has yet seen the wisdom of my plan, so I decided to by-pass the Christmas table altogether and unload *A Sackful of Limericks* straight onto your pile of presents. They're written to appeal to all those who run out of things to unwrap. Now, instead of looking sad and unloved, they can fight back by reciting a limerick or ten, entertaining, irritating and annoying all those who are slowly amassing socks, homemade jams and pruning shears. They can also be used when Grandad wakes up, or the computer goes down, or to get rid of unwanted guests. They can also be used to help digestion, frighten the cat, and break the ice when the vicar calls.

I've written them over the years, and many were originally published as a collection for children. I feel, though, that limericks are ageless. By which I mean that it's impossible to put an age limit on them. The form of a limerick has a certain melody to it, which, if you get it right, is something to which people of all ages can respond. It's also infuriatingly impossible to stop writing them once you've got the flow, which is why there are a lot in this collection which have not previously seen the light of day.

So, with these confessions from a compulsive Limericist out of the way, it only remains for me to thank Caroline Roberts of Hutchinson who encouraged, nagged and generally cajoled me into the first published selection, Susan Sandon and Nigel Wilcockson at Random House for picking up the baton and inspiring me to add to the sackful, and my original and wonderful illustrator Tony Ross for coming on board again and bringing to life the weird collection of those who live in these limericks.

Michael Palin
London
May 2016

Author's note to the first edition

There is no easy way to write limericks. The age-old formula of standing in a bucket of Mersey water with a kilt worn inside out is still not popular. There are those who swear by electrodes taped to the head and others who think that carrots eaten from the thick end downwards on the third Sunday of any month with an 's' in it are most effective, but for me there's nothing to beat a very large Scotch, a shoulder massage and an editor who rings every half-hour to see how it's going. But sometimes nothing works.

I have sadly had to abandon certain limericks such as the one about the fellow from Grantham called Titus who was

> *A boon to all limerick writers,*
> *The number of times*
> *His name could make rhymes*
> *Was practically ad infinitus.*

on the grounds of bad Latin; and the young man from Vermont

> *Who had all that a young man could want*
> *Nice clothes, lots of cash,*
> *A non-serious rash,*
> *Except both legs were on back to front,*

as it didn't rhyme; and the policeman from Tring

> *Who had an extraordinary thing*

But I did manage to write a limerick for a nice lady called Paula who said she was a midwife and no one ever wrote limericks about midwives:

> *They said of a midwife called Paula,*
> *If there was any trouble just call her.*
> *Her skills in the water*
> *She learnt from a porter,*
> *Who delivered fish, fresh, off a trawler.*

Happy reading.

A Sackful of Limericks

A doctor from near Aberdeen
Had a pet anaconda called Jean.
If you said, 'Please',
She'd give you a squeeze
But few of the patients were keen.

A garage mechanic called Knowles
Had more than his fair share of holes.
He had two in each ear
And four more quite near
And nostrils the size of bread rolls.

A young man from Redcar, called Vince
Used to drop very obvious hints
Like, 'Oh dear, I *say!*
It's my *birthday* today
And I'm right out of After Eight mints.'

A deep-water sailor called Rod
Used to dive in and rescue live cod.
He wasn't a fool
Who thought nets were cruel,
But he certainly was pretty odd.

A banker from Ealing called Stott
Awoke with a terrible spot.
Though he put on some plaster
It only grew faster
And at work it went off like a shot.

There once was a fellow called Lake
Whose motives were somewhat opaque.
He'd give you a punch,
Then take you to lunch,
And pretend that his kneecaps were fake.

An eccentric landowner called Grey
Spent Christmas a very strange way.
Instead of nice presents
He'd give people pheasants,
And laugh as they all flew away.

There was a young man called O'Toole,
Who, when he saw food, used to drool;
Pizza, mangoes or tripe,
Avocado, when ripe –
Even gruel made his drool form a pool.

A couple from Ruislip called Fryer
Had a boat called *The Wings of Desire*.
They sailed the canals
With a boatload of pals
And the cream of the local school choir.

A troubled young fellow called Henshall
Came over all existential.
He went to a shrink
Who led him to think
That nothing was really essential.

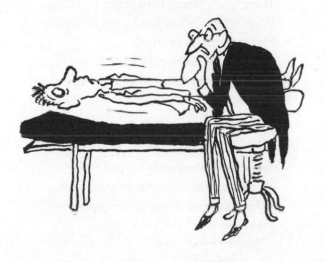

There was a young vicar from Usk
Whose wife had an elephant's tusk.
Too big for the shed
It went under the bed
And only came out after dusk.

A Frenchman called Didier Brume
Had a clear premonition of doom.
So, to hasten his death,
He just held his breath,
And lay, all alone, on a tomb.

An eccentric accountant called Gaines
Much preferred starters to mains.
He'd have soup and then soup
And after that, soup,
And a very small portion of brains.

There once was a deck-hand called Chris
Who quite enjoyed taking the piss.
He stood up and roared,
'Man overboard!'
When the victim was clearly a Miss.

A young trainee vicar called Steve
So enjoyed himself one Christmas Eve
That he spent Christmas Day
On the West Sussex Way
Doing things you'd never believe.

A clever young schoolboy from Leicester
Allowed a sore finger to fester.
It doubled in size,
And the sound of his cries
Could be heard from as far off as Chester.

A cross-country runner called Bert
Put in a last-minute spurt.
He shot past the leader
And into a feeder,
So the last hundred yards really hurt.

There once was a fellow called Santa
Who was ever so proud of his banter.
He'd put on a voice
And call himself Joyce
And make silly calls to Atlanta.

A promising athlete called Noel
Got his vaulting pole stuck in the hole.
He flew through the air
But his pole just stayed there
And now sadly he's back on the dole.

A young TV star from Jamaica
Had a stormy affair with a baker.
He had the show
And she had the dough,
But she gave it all up for a Quaker.

An elderly man from Nantucket
Kept his wife in a very large bucket,
His son in a tin,
His dog in a bin,
And nobody knows how they stuck it.

A big bearded fellow called Sparks
Got up to all manner of larks.
He'd sing Christmas carols
While standing on barrels
In some of the best London parks.

There once was a dachshund called Clive
Who was wanted dead or alive
For biting pet cats
And swallowing bats
And attacking queen bees in their hive.

A young fashion model from Lille
Was addicted to hot jellied eel.
Not just one now and then
But eight, sometimes ten,
Which greatly reduced her appeal.

A chair-lift attendant called Frank
Ate tropical fish from a tank.
When he'd swallowed them whole,
He picked up a bowl
Of goldfish beside them, and drank.

A batsman from Sydney called Fairlie
Hit a very fast ball good and squarely.
A fielder called Reith
Caught the ball in his teeth –
A thing which he did very rarely.

A lady I met in Devizes
Bought knickers in all sorts of sizes:
Number 10 for her dad,
Number 3 for the lad,
And the rest she kept for disguises.

A young cocker spaniel called Spur
Became quite addicted to myrrh.
He didn't like gold –
He found it too cold –
And frankincense stuck in his fur.

A lady musician called Hamp
Was prone to quite severe cramp.
One day at the harp
She got stuck in F-sharp,
And was freed by acetylene lamp.

A javelin thrower called Vicky
Found the grip of her javelin sticky.
When it came to the throw
She couldn't let go –
Making judging the distance quite tricky.

A brave taxi driver called Clive
Once found a black mamba alive.
Though they said, 'Shoot it dead!'
He decided instead
To take it round town for a drive.

A young man from Grimsby called Short
Used to give things a great deal of thought –
Like, Is there a God?
And, How long's a cod?
And, Is stamp collecting a sport?

There was a young lady called Ben
Who got on ever so well with the men.
It wasn't the beard
Or the way that she cheered
But the pipe that she smoked now and then.

There once was a fellow called Keith
Who wore nothing at all underneath.
When asked was that wise
For a man of his size,
He muttered abuse through clenched teeth.

An unemployed dentist called Hodge
Rolled used cotton wool in a wodge,
Which he fired, with some force,
From the back of a horse,
Causing elderly people to dodge.

A carpenter's helper called Neville
Never made anything level.
A table or chair
Was best made elsewhere,
Then taken to Neville to bevel.

A lady from Florence called Nella
Had a dog that was such a good smeller
It could sniff out a meal
From as far off as Lille,
And if it was nice it would tell her.

A pretty young lady called Splatt
Was mistaken one day for a cat
By a man called Van Damm
Who made pets into jam –
And now she's spread out rather flat.

A wealthy young lady called Smirke
Spent much of her time with a Turk.
He ran a small shop
With a room at the top
Where he made all kinds of things work.

There once was a man called O'Brien
Who, whatever he did, kept his tie on:
In the shower, or deck chair,
He was heard to declare
That 'It shows I'm a man to rely on!'

There was a gravedigger from Barnes
Whose clothes were all covered in darns.
He'd dug fewer holes
In his life, for poor souls,
Than his sweater had under the arms.

A kindly old fellow called Clore
Gave all that he had to the poor;
But, alas and alack,
They would not give it back,
So he's not giving them any more.

A surgeon from Glasgow called Mac,
Once forgot to put everything back.
As his train made to start,
His case came apart,
And a kidney rolled down off the rack.

A fellow from Bristol, called Neve,
Was seriously known to believe
That the world being flat,
If once lost, your cat
Would be terribly hard to retrieve.

An hotelier, name of O'Rourke,
Once had a quail that could talk.
It would make little nests,
And shout at the guests,
And warn against eating the pork.

A very light sleeper called Lowndes
Would wake at the slightest of sounds,
Like a fish thinking hard,
Or the rustling of lard,
Or moles far beneath football grounds.

A handsome young fellow called Lance
Had over a hundred great-aunts.
He kept some in drawers
And some under floors,
And the judge never gave him a chance.

A nervous young lady called Hughes
Never knew quite what to choose.
The harder she'd try
The less she knew why,
Or whether, and if so, then whose?

There once was a man from Dubai,
And to this day no one knows why
He stood on his head,
Slowly spun round, and said,
'EeDiggity Obleson Rye!'

There once was a man from Malaya
Who refused to pay his bus fare
          (pronounced *fay-er*)
On account of the fact
That the downstairs was packed
And the upstairs reserved for the Mayor.
          (pronounced *may-er*)

*(The author would like to thank readers for their
help with this limerick.)*

There was a young fellow from Wapping
Who found two live slugs in his shopping.
The girl at the till
Took them both off the bill,
And went on to the next without stopping.

There once was a vicar from Bude
Whose manners at table were rude.
It wasn't the noise,
As he ate saveloys,
But the way that he sat on his food.

There was a fishmonger from Leeds
Whose children were all complete weeds –
The sight of a cod
Or anything odd
Would make them go weak at the kneeds.

A young man from Utah, called Paul,
Had a head several sizes too small.
For the price of a dollar
He'd loosen his collar
And show how far down it could fall.

There was a young fellow called Pringle
Who desperately wished to stay single.
But as soon as he saw
One young lady, or more,
He was filled with a strong urge to mingle.

There was a young man from Malta,
Who bought his grandfather an altar,
But, as happens to most,
It broke in the post,
As it squeezed through the Straits of Gibraltar.

A nervous young woman called Fay
Always used to react with dismay
At a match being struck,
Or the quack of a duck.
'Hello, Fay!' made her faint clean away.

There once was a fellow called West
Who found it quite hard to get dressed.
He used to quite dread
Putting socks on his head
And getting both legs through his vest.

There once was a man from Manila
Who christened his young son Attila.
It was only in fun –
But he grew up a Hun,
Renowned through the world as a killer.

A singer related to Brahms
Showed an ambulance driver her charms.
He liked them so much
He allowed her to touch
The knob that set off the alarms.

A lady from near Milton Keynes
Had trouble digesting her greens.
The odd Brussels sprout
Would find its way out,
But the greens that brought screams
  were French beans.

A young shipping clerk from Port Said
Was found with his arms and legs tied
Inside an old trunk
That belonged to a monk
To whom, for advice, he'd applied.

A young mountaineer called Vic
Became quite close friends with a stick.
He took it for walks,
And they had little talks,
Then it left him to live with a brick.

A young man from Berwick-on-Tweed
Kept a very strange thing on a lead.
He was never once seen
To give it a clean
Or anything else it might need.

There once was a fellow called Maude
Who became very easily bored,
One day, at a lunch,
He fell in a bunch
Of lupins, and lay there, ignored.

There was a young fellow called Lloyd
Who everyone tried to avoid.
It wasn't the smell,
Or the stories he'd tell,
But the way he pronounced Betws-y-Coed.

(Author's note: *This limerick will work best for
experienced Welsh speakers.*)

An Ilford dog-trainer called Mellish
Made a miniature poodle's life hellish.
It was thought well deserved
When a dog so reserved
One night ate him, with evident relish.

A man from the north, called Adair,
When he washed, never took proper care:
At first it was spots,
Then rashes, then lots
Of patches of unwanted hair.

An arm-wrestling vicar from Looe
Invited some friends to a do.
Dressed only in shorts,
He taught them some sports
They thought very few vicars knew.

A young discus-thrower called Earl
Could not take his eyes off a girl,
Which is rather bad luck –
With them hopelessly stuck
He can no longer see where to hurl.

There was a young man from Kashmir
Who shouted, one day, 'Over here!'
But from so far away
That he's still there today,
And will be for ever, I fear.

A curious fellow called Stoat
Bought jewellery and things for a goat.
For favours like these
It gave milk and cheese
And kicked him one day in the throat.

There once was a tortoise called Joe
Whose progress was painfully slow.
He'd stop for a week,
Look around, take a peek,
Then unlike a shot, off he'd go.

There once was a camper called Jack
Who found a huge snake in his pack.
He cut it in two,
Gave half to the zoo,
And then put the other half back.

A peculiar fellow called Long
Once sat on a very sharp prong.
He gave a great shout –
As his friends pulled it out.
Then he sat on the next one along.

A man by the name of Geneen
Was asked by his wife where he'd been.
He *Ummed* and he *Ahhhed* –
So she hit him, quite hard,
On the head, with a large soup tureen.

A handsome young fellow called Miles
Used to help pretty girls over stiles.
Once over the top
One or two used to stop,
But the rest kept on going for Miles.

A curious lady called Davies
Used to make threatening phone calls to Avis.
She'd pretend to be mad,
And ask if they had
Any cars called Lucinda or Mavis.

An excitable fellow called Gomez
Told his dog 'I don' wanna *no* mess.
Cleaning the floor
I ain't doin' no more,
And I've had it with nasty aromas.'

A young scuba-diver called Jeff
Was so good at holding his breff
He could swim anywhere
On a lungful of air
Which scared his poor muvver to deff.

A Tory backbencher called Sandys
Detested the sound of brass bandys.
When they started to play
He'd run far away,
And cover his head with his handys.

(Author's note: *Ask an aged relative how to pronounce 'Sandys'*)

A lodger from Brighton called Briggs
Had a penchant for syrup of figs;
Though he did what he could,
The results were so good
He had to keep moving his digs.

A mother from Seascale called Pippa
Found some nuclear waste in a kipper.
When she told them she'd found it,
They said, 'Eat around it,
And keep it away from the nipper.'

A curious young man from Calcutta
Was known as a bit of a nutter.
After prawn vindaloo
And a Guinness or two
He'd lie, very still, in the gutter.

A handsome young fellow called Frears
Was attracted to girls by their ears.
He'd traverse the globe
For a really nice lobe,
And the sight would reduce him to tears.

There was a young lady called Marge
Who liked men with features quite large.
Her long line of suitors
Had whacking great hooters,
Apart from a Monsieur Lafarge.

There once was a fellow called Scaggs,
Who kept all his things in black bags.
When people asked why,
He'd admit, with a sigh,
There were certainly all sorts of snags.

A South African farmer called Ted
Attacked a brick wall with his head.
The blow could be felt,
All over the veldt,
And in less than an hour he was dead.

The Penarth Double Limerick

A fisherman's wife from Penarth
Invented a new way to laugh,
Using both of her feet
And a long rubber sheet
Which her son folded neatly in half.

When she felt a good joke coming on,
She'd shout, 'Get the rubber sheet, John!'
But when it was found
And laid out on the ground
Whatever was funny had gone.

One day in a small town on Skye
A finger turned up in a pie,
Then a nose and two lips,
Then a fine pair of hips,
Then a waitress jumped out and said, 'Hi!'

An impetuous Welshman called Caine
Threw some half-eaten fish from a train.
It struck an MP
Which, I'm sure you'll agree,
Showed a truly impeccable aim.

A refuse collector called Bert
Had a priceless collection of dirt
Covered up by a screen
To keep it all clean,
With a guard dog on constant alert.

An optician who practised in Rye
Sadly had only one eye.
He'd given the other
To somebody's brother,
And it wasn't the thing to ask why.

There was a young fellow called Priestley,
Whose behaviour to women was beastly.
He'd promise them wine
And a jolly good time –
Then give them a weekend in Eastleigh.

A very smart lady from Rye
Had an accent that gave her awyc.
She said she was posh,
Which they all knew was tosh –
She came from East Ham, so they sye.

A cartoonist from Worksop, called Botts,
Tied himself in such intricate knots
That even his friends
Could not find the ends,
And he died, still unravelled, in Notts.

A Sussex fast bowler called Lyall
Took a run-up of nearly a mile.
In one Gillette Cup
He never turned up –
And was last seen just south of the Nile.

A young ballet dancer called Bruce
Wore tights that were rather too loose.
As he leapt through the air
All his skills were laid bare,
And his face went a very bright puce.

An ageing shot-putter called Carl
Used to pull back his lips in a snarl,
Revealing, beneath,
Several rows of white teeth
And a bridge he'd had fitted in Arles.

A greedy young fellow called Wrench
Owned a cat, two small dogs, and a tench.
One day, in a trice,
He cooked them with rice,
And called the dish something in French.

A jolly old fellow called Boakes
Knew five thousand eight hundred jokes,
Which, ranging from bad
To the dismally sad,
He tried out on helpless old folks.

There once was a poet called Sime
Who avoided the obvious rhyme.
He put 'this' after 'that',
And 'dog' after 'cat',
And he hated this sort of last line.

A Wrexham tattooist called Ken
Used to draw little pictures on men;
Sometimes a still life,
Or another man's wife,
Or, once in a while, Tony Benn.

A curious fellow called Lamb
Used to shout things at old tins of Spam
Like, 'You silly old tin!'
And, 'Where have *you* been?'
Then he'd move on and rubbish the jam.

A trainee magician called Mick
Made a frightful mistake with a trick,
When he turned a small boy,
His mum's pride and joy,
Irreversibly into a brick.

There was a young fellow called Clem
Who possessed quite remarkable phlegm:
When he once by mistake
Choked to death on a cake,
He got up and did it again.

There was a young fellow called Grist
Who found the girls hard to resist.
He'd give them the eye,
But was so deeply shy
That he always just missed being kissed.

A highly-strung lady called Weems,
Once caught a man in her dreams.
He vanished away
In the cold light of day –
But he left her some peppermint creams.

A veterinary surgeon from Fife
Once dressed up to frighten his wife.
When asked, 'Is it wise?'
He replied in surprise,
'Where I come from this sort of thing's rife.'

A lady from Louth with a lisp
Liked her sausages specially crisp.
But in trying to say
That she liked them that way
She covered her friends in a mitht.

An earnest young lady called Soames
Wrote a very large book about gnomes;
But the tales were so tall
And the sales were so small
She was left with huge unwanted tomes.

There once was a fellow called Doyle
Who covered up people with soil
Long before they were dead –
Which would make them seem red,
And bring quite placid chaps to the boil.

A gravedigger's helper called Maddox
Was obsessed with an urge to ride haddocks.
He made little paddles,
And waterproof saddles,
But the fish never stayed in the paddocks.

A lady from Brighton called Palmer
Became quite an expert snake charmer.
The snakes called her Miss,
And gave a loud hiss
When it looked as if someone would harm her.

A research biochemist from Goring
Found cricketers rather alluring.
He'd turn up at the match
And hope for a catch
Or something a bit more enduring.

A lady from Bristol called Bligh,
Who all of her life had been shy,
Was cured in a week
By two Poles and a Greek
Whom she met on the Island of Skye.

There once was a teacher called Fox,
Who kept something rare in a box.
One night, as dawn broke,
The creature awoke
And ran off with his shoes and his socks.

A Yorkshireman living in Worcester
Said to his wife, 'Fetch a duster.
This table from Hull
Has gone ever so dull.
A duster will bring back its lustre.'

(To be read only in a Yorkshire accent.)

There once was a fellow called God,
Whom everyone thought rather odd.
Apart from a lady,
Called Eileen O'Grady,
Who worshipped the ground that he trod.

A fisherman living in York
Complained that the length of the walk
From his house to the sea
Took two days or three,
And more if he stopped for a talk.

There was a young man from Melrose
Who had a large thing on his nose,
One on his back,
And three in a sack,
And four between each of his toes.

A handsome young German called Fritz,
On seeing a friend do the splits,
With a triumphant cry,
Shouted, 'Here, let me try!'
And broke into two equal bits.

There once was a lady called Tate
Who won a live bear at a fete.
To her home it was led,
But it hadn't been fed,
And the police got there seconds too late.

A vicar from Esher called Hughes
Used to greatly enjoy a quick snooze
At lunchtime or tea,
If the pulpit was free,
And if not, he'd kip in the pews.

A man called O'Hara one day
Decided he'd make the world pay.
He wrote down a plan
To destroy every man –
But the wind came and blew it away.

A young man from Beccles, called Duke,
Discovered one day, by a fluke,
If he put on a fez
And a little pince-nez
He looked like the young King Farouk.

A young mountaineer from Nepal
Invented a new way to fall.
It worked out so well
That no one could tell
Where he was – if he'd landed at all.

When asked tricky questions old Riley
Would simply reply, very drily,
'I'm sorry, old bean,
I don't know what you mean,'
Then sidle off home, smiling wryly.

A chiropodist – friends call her Dawn –
Used to do people's feet on her lawn;
But the neighbours complained
When a lady, unnamed,
Was hit in the eye by a corn.

A travelling salesman called Lloyd
Was known as a man to avoid.
The horrified stares
As he showed off his wares
Was a sight that he clearly enjoyed.

There was a young fellow called Ben,
Who angered his friends now and then
By running up stairs
And shouting, 'Who cares?'
Then doing the whole thing again.

A girl from Carlisle called Lucy
One day came over all goosy.
Although it seemed strange,
She got used to the change,
And by Christmas was really quite juicy.

A white cocker spaniel from Poole
Had a thing about Peter O'Toole.
When he came on the telly,
He'd roll on his belly
And do funny things to the stool.

There was a young man called Potter,
Whose girlfriend resembled an otter –
About three feet long,
Smooth fur, fairly strong:
No one quite liked to ask where he'd got her.

There was a young fellow called Owen
Who had to keep goin' and goin'.
Psychiatrists said
Being dropped on his head
Had caused all the toin' and froin'.

A strange man called Ron took a bet:
He'd swim three lengths without getting wet.
With commendable cool,
He emptied the pool,
Dived in, and he's not come round yet.

There was a surveyor from Kent
Whose theodolite got rather bent.
The result you can see
On the A423,
Which never goes quite where they meant.

A boxer from Malta called Raymon
Used a big concrete wall to take aim on.
He broke both his arms
And three lucky charms –
One with his grandmother's name on.

An aspiring young MP from Tring
Invented a very neat thing.
He created a voter,
Complete with a motor,
Which he found would support anything.

A curious young fellow named Kurt
Used to climb Alpine peaks in a skirt.
He said it felt nice
In the snow and the ice,
And it kept those below more alert.

A curious man named McGraw
Caught part of his head in a door.
When he came back next week
With his wife, who was Greek,
He found it, still there, on the floor.

There was a young fellow called Kamp
Who sunbathed in his loo with a lamp.
But a flash in the pan
Gave him more than a tan –
The result of the wires getting damp.

An elderly lady from Fleet
Once scored a goal with both feet,
And, despite her great age,
Earns a reasonable wage
As reserve centre forward for Crete.

A butcher's assistant called Phil
Was caught with his hands in the till.
He tried to cut meat
Using only his feet
But the sight made the customers ill.

A dog from Sri Lanka called Patch
Sat down on a tree stump to scratch;
But he found that the flea,
Was not one, but three,
And the first of a very large batch.

There was a young man from the Cape
Who swallowed his hat for a jape.
It was easy to tell
Why he felt so unwell
By his stomach's extraordinary shape.

A retired metal-worker called Noades
Used to solve little problems for toads,
Like where to jump next,
Or a hard Latin text,
Or how to avoid major roads.

A man on a length of elastic
Decided to do something drastic.
When he jumped off the cliff he
Came back in a jiffy,
And screamed to his friends, 'It's fantastic!'

A sensitive boy named McKay
Let out the most terrible cry
When he found something shocking
Inside of his stocking
That was slimy and green and could fly.

A little boy spied Santa Claus
Escaping the shop on all fours.
After hours in the grotto
He'd got a bit blotto,
And was heading, quite fast, for the doors.

There once was an author called Palin,
For whom limericks seemed just plain sailin',
He wrote ninety-four*
But when asked for one more,
He just ran down the street screaming,
  'Leave me alone!'

(Author's note: *One hundred and fifty-five, actually, but you
try and rhyme that with 'more'!*)